LET'S GO Phonics

2

Jeffrey D. Lehman

OXFORD
UNIVERSITY PRESS

OXFORD
UNIVERSITY PRESS

198 Madison Avenue
New York, NY 10016 USA

Great Clarendon Street, Oxford OX2 6DP UK

Oxford University Press is a department of the University of Oxford.
It furthers the University's objective of excellence in research, scholarship,
and education by publishing worldwide in

Oxford New York

Auckland Cape Town Dar es Salaam Hong Kong Karachi
Kuala Lumpur Madrid Melbourne Mexico City Nairobi
New Delhi Shanghai Taipei Toronto

With offices in

Argentina Austria Brazil Chile Czech Republic France Greece
Guatemala Hungary Italy Japan Poland Portugal Singapore
South Korea Switzerland Thailand Turkey Ukraine Vietnam

OXFORD and OXFORD ENGLISH are registered trademarks of
Oxford University Press

Senior Editor: Paul Phillips
Editor: Kathryn L. O'Dell
Art Director: Maj-Britt Hagsted
Design Project Manager: Amelia L. Carling
Senior Designer: Stacy Merlin (cover)
Production Manager: Shanta Persaud
Production Controller: Eve Wong

Page layout and art buying by Delgado and Company, Inc.

ISBN-13: 978 0 19 439507 6
ISBN-10: 0 19 439507 3
ISBN-13: 13: 978 0 19 439510 6
ISBN-10: 0 19 439510 3
ISBN-13: 978 0 19 439513 7
ISBN-10: 0 19 439513 8

Printed in Hong Kong.

10 9 8 7 6 5 4 3 2 1

Acknowledgments:

Cover Illustration by: Bob Berry Illustration

Bob Berry Illustration: 8, 9, 11, 12, 14, 15, 20, 22, 24, 26, 28, 29, 33, 34, 36,
37, 39, 40, 45, 46, 48, 49, 51, 52, 54, 55, 57, 58; Susie Lee Jin: 23, 25, 27, 33,
35, 57; Christine Schneider: 8, 24, 33, 49, 53; Steve Henry: 15, 40, 47, 50,
54; Priscilla Burris: 10, 29, 37, 39, 51; Sharon Harmer: 11, 22, 23, 38, 57;
Mary Hall: 22, 27, 34, 46; Kevin Brown/Top Dog Studio: 9, 15, 47, 55; Mircea
Catusanu: 36, 45, 53, 56; Rita Lascaro: 11, 25, 45, 59; Chris Reed: 9, 24, 26, 48;
Laura Freeman-Hines: 20, 21, 28, 50; Dana Regan: 10, 35, 37, 55; Ken Bowser:
21, 40, 41; Sarah Dillard: 12, 29, 58; Tammie Lyon: 12, 14, 58; Jane Smith:
48, 52, 59; Jim Haynes: 8, 46, 52; Elizabeth Di Gregorio: 51, 54; Tim Webb
Illustration: 26, 41; Terri and Joe Chicko: 13, 56; Teresa Anderko: 13, 36;
Nancy Munger: 14, 34; Nelle Davis/Craven Design: 16, 39

Table of Contents

General Review

A. Begins with b or p. Listen and write. 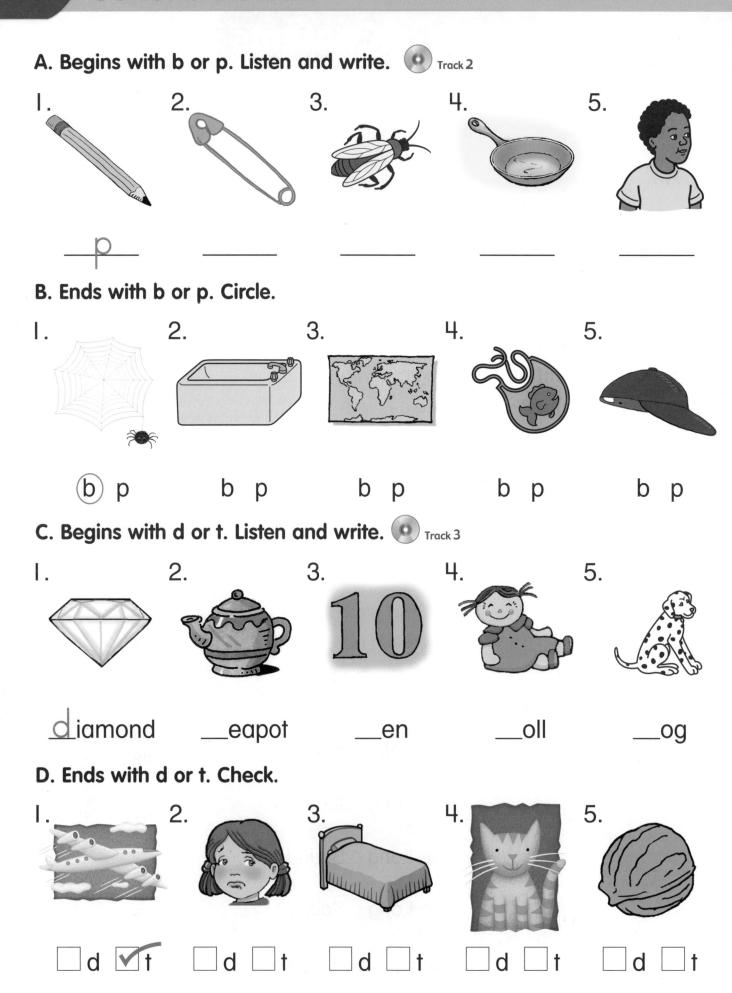 Track 2

1. ___p___
2. _____
3. _____
4. _____
5. _____

B. Ends with b or p. Circle.

1. (b) p
2. b p
3. b p
4. b p
5. b p

C. Begins with d or t. Listen and write. Track 3

1. d̲iamond
2. ___eapot
3. ___en
4. ___oll
5. ___og

D. Ends with d or t. Check.

1. ☐ d ☑ t
2. ☐ d ☐ t
3. ☐ d ☐ t
4. ☐ d ☐ t
5. ☐ d ☐ t

E. Begins with f or v. Circle the words with the same sound.

1. **f**ox

2. **v**an

F. Ends with the f or v sound. Write.

1.	2.	3.	4.	5.

lea__	fi__e	di__e	hoo__	hi__e

G. Begins with m or n. Write.

1.	2.	3.	4.	5.

_____	_____	_____	_____	_____

H. Ends with m or n. Listen and circle. Track 4

1.	2.	3.	4.	5.

m n	m n	m n	m n	m n

I. Short a or e. Write.

1. _ gg

2. r _ d

3. m _ p

4. p _ n

5. c _ t

J. Short e or i. Check.

1. ☐ e ☐ i

2. ☐ e ☐ i

3. ☐ e ☐ i

4. ☐ e ☐ i

5. ☐ e ☐ i

K. Short a and i. Circle the words that rhyme.

1. hat

2. wig

L. Short i or o. Listen and check. 🔘 Track 5

1. ☐ i ☐ o

2. ☐ i ☐ o

3. ☐ i ☐ o

4. ☐ i ☐ o

5. ☐ i ☐ o

M. Short o or u. Listen and write. 🔘 Track 6

1.

__melet

2.

__mbrella

3.

b__g

4.

__om

5.

d__ck

N. h or j. Circle.

1.

h   j

2.

h   j

3.

h   j

4.

h   j

5.

h   j

O. Hard g or soft g. Listen and circle. 🔘 Track 7

1.

hard g
soft g

2.

hard g
soft g

3.

hard g
soft g

4.

hard g
soft g

5.

hard g
soft g

P. Begins or ends with hard g. Listen and write. 🔘 Track 8

1.

__ | g

2.

__ | __

3.

__ | __

4.

__ | __

5.

__ | __

Q. Hard c or soft c. Listen and circle. 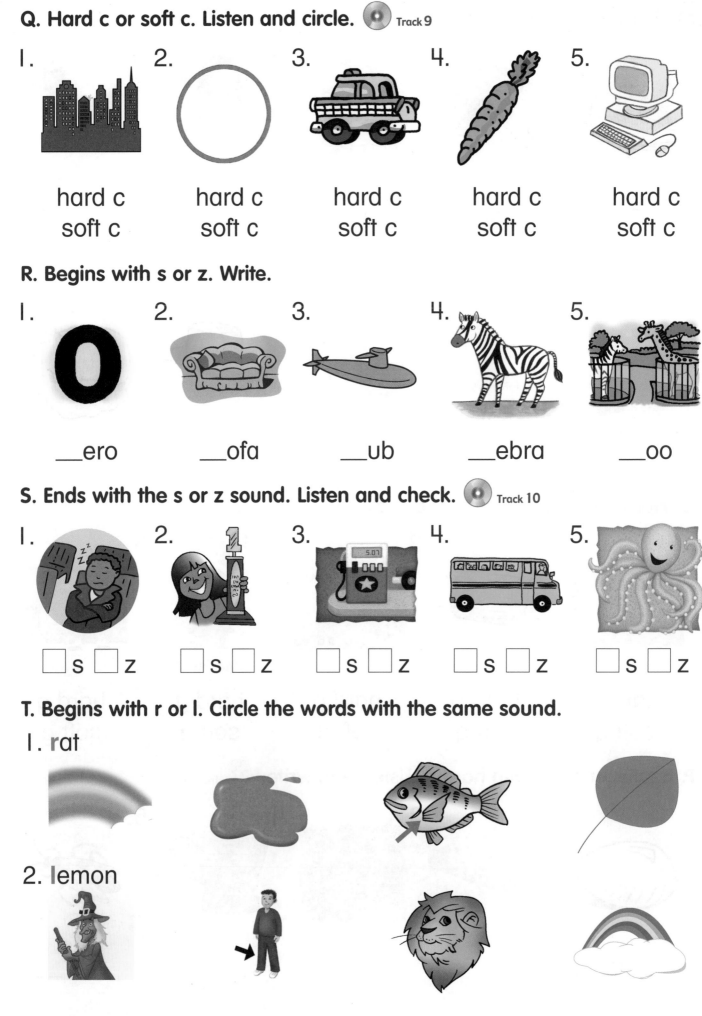 Track 9

1.

hard c
soft c

2.

hard c
soft c

3.

hard c
soft c

4.

hard c
soft c

5.

hard c
soft c

R. Begins with s or z. Write.

1.

__ero

2.

__ofa

3.

__ub

4.

__ebra

5.

__oo

S. Ends with the s or z sound. Listen and check. Track 10

1.

☐ s ☐ z

2.

☐ s ☐ z

3.

☐ s ☐ z

4.

☐ s ☐ z

5.

☐ s ☐ z

T. Begins with r or l. Circle the words with the same sound.

1. rat

2. lemon

U. Ends with r or l. Check.

1.
2.
3.
4.
5.

☐ r ☐ l ☐ r ☐ l ☐ r ☐ l ☐ r ☐ l ☐ r ☐ l

V. Begins with w or y. Write.

1.
2.
3
4.
5.

_____ _____ _____ _____ _____

W. Ends with k or x. Listen and circle. Track 11

1.
2.
3.
4.
5.

k x   k x   k x   k x   k x

X. Begins with k or qu. Write.

1.
2.
3.
4.
5.

__iet   __ing   __een   __ey   __ail

Let's Learn

A. Listen and speak. Track 12

black

blob

cloud

clock

flag

flip

Let's Practice

A. Write.

<u>bl</u>ack

____ock

____ip

B. Listen and color. Track 13

 = cl   = bl   ⭐ = fl

1.
☆

2.
☆

3.
☆

4.
☆

5.
☆

Let's Learn

glue

glass

plum

plug

slam

slug

Let's Practice

A. Write.

____ue

____ug

____am

B. Listen and match. Track 15

| pl = begins with pl | gl = begins with gl | sl = begins with sl |

pl

gl

sl

1.

2.

3.

4.

5.

Let's Choose

A. Write bl, cl, fl, gl, pl, or sl.

1.
fl

2.
___

3.
___

4.
___

5.
___

6.
___

7.
___

8.
___

Let's Read

A. Read. Then write.

1. I see a slim slug slip.

2. I see a class of clams clap.

3. I see a flower on a flat flag.

4. I see a blue and black blob.

bl	cl	fl	sl
1. blue	1. _____	1. _____	1. _____
2. _____	2. _____	2. _____	2. _____
3. _____	3. _____	3. _____	3. _____

br fr cr dr

Let's Learn

A. Listen and speak. Track 16

brush

bread

crib

crayon

draw

dress

frog

friend

Let's Practice

A. Write.

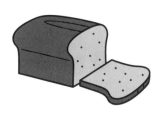   

____ead   ____ayon   ____ess   ____iend

B. Listen. Write dr, fr, br, or cr. Track 17

1.    2.    3.    4.    5.

____   ____   ____   ____   ____

Let's Learn

A. Listen and speak. Track 18

grin

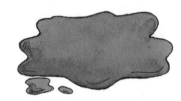

green

present

princess

train

tree

Let's Practice

A. Write.

____in

____incess

____ain

B. Listen and draw. Track 19

◯ = begins with **pr**　　△ = begins with **tr**　　▢ = begins with **gr**

1.
2.
3.
4.
5.

Let's Choose

A. Write br, cr, dr, fr, gr, pr, or tr.

1.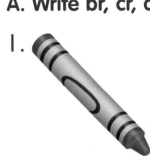

_____

2.

_____

3.

_____

4.

_____

5.

_____

6.

_____

7.

_____

8.

_____

Let's Read

A. Write and read.

1.

2.

3.

4.

a	**gr**een	d	**cr**ab	f	**br**other	h	**pr**incess
b	**fr**og	e	**gr**ass	g	**dr**um	i	**tr**ee
c	**dr**aws						

1. A ^a green ^b_____ ^c_____.

2. The ^d_____ is on the ^e_____.

3. A ^f_____ plays the ^g_____.

4. The ^h_____ is in the ⁱ_____.

sc sm
sn

Let's Learn

A. Listen and speak. Track 20

scarf   scare   smell

smile   snow   snail

Let's Practice

A. Write.

sc   sm   sn

____uba   ____ar   ____og   ____all   ____ake   ____iff

B. Listen and circle. Track 21

1.

   sc   sn (sm)

2.

   sc   sn   sm

3.

   sc   sn   sm

4.

   sc   sn   sm

5.

   sc   sn   sm

6.

   sc   sn   sm

Let's Learn

A. Listen and speak. Track 22

sky

spill

stir

swim

Let's Practice

A. Write.

sk

____unk

____i

sp

____ot

B-O-Y

____ell

st

____ar

____omach

sw

____ing

____at

B. Listen and color. Track 23

 = sk   = sp   ♥ = st   ♡ = sw

1.
♥

2.
♡

3.
♡

4.
♡

5.
♡

6.
♡

7.
♡

8.
♡

Let's Choose

A. Listen and circle. Track 24

1.

   sm sp

2.

   sc st

3.

   sn sw

4.

   sc sp

B. Listen. Write sk, sm, sn, sp, st, or sw. Track 25

1.

   _____

2.

   _____

3.

   _____

4.

   _____

5.

   _____

6.

   _____

7.

   _____

8.

   _____

Let's Read

A. Read and draw.

1. The **st**ar is in **sp**ace.

2. The **sm**all **sk**unk is in the **sn**ow.

1.

2.

A. bl, cl, fl, gl, pl, or sl. Circle.

1.

bl cl fl

2.

bl cl fl

3.

bl cl fl

4.

bl cl fl

5.

bl cl fl

6.

gl pl sl

7.

gl pl sl

8.

gl pl sl

9.

gl pl sl

10.

gl pl sl

B. br or cr. Circle the words with the same sound.

1. **br**ush

2. **cr**ib

C. fr, dr, or gr. Write.

1.

__ass

2.

__een

3.

__aw

4.

__og

5.

__um

D. pr, tr, or dr. Write.

1.

2.

3.

4.

5.

_____ _____ _____ _____ _____

E. sc, sm, or sn. Circle.

1.

2.

3.

4.

5.

sc sm sn   sc sm sn   sc sm sn   sc sm sn   sc sm sn

F. sk or sp. Circle the words with the same sound.

1. **sk**unk

2. **sp**ot

G. st or sw. Write.

1.

2.

3.

4.

5.

___im   ___ar   ___an   ___ir   ___op

H. Write.

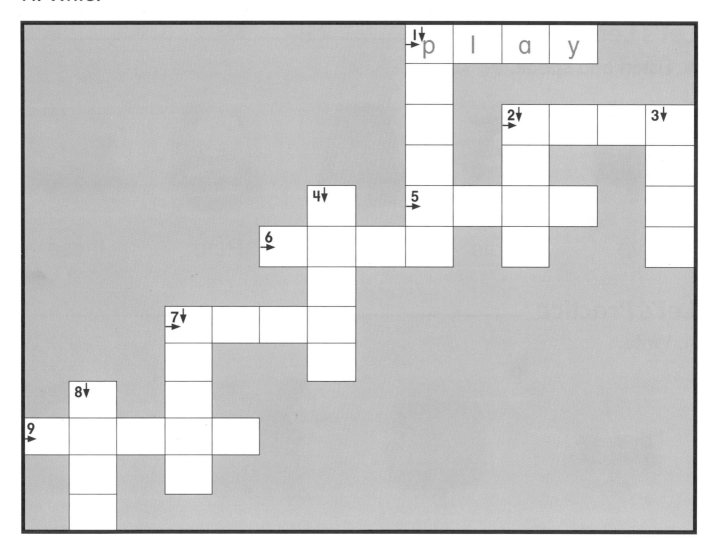

ACROSS

1. 2. 5. 6. 7. 9.

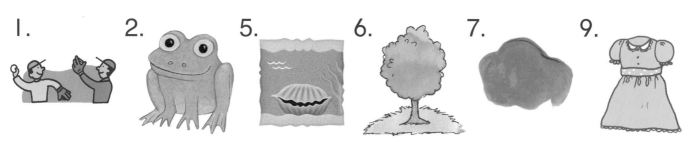

DOWN

1. 2. 3. 4. 7. 8.

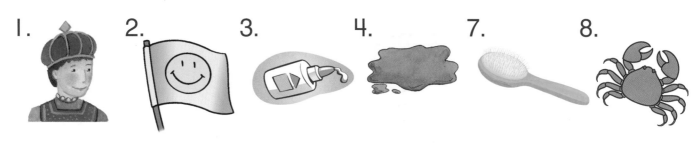

Magic e with a and e

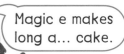

> Magic e makes long a... cake.

> Magic e makes long e... Pete.

Let's Learn

A. Listen and speak. Track 26

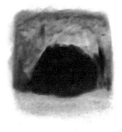

cave   whale   cape   Pete   these

Let's Practice

A. Write.

1.

c a k e

2.

l__k__

3.

th__s__

4.

P__t__

B. Listen. Circle the magic e with a words. Track 27

1.

2.

3.

4.

5.

C. Listen. Color the magic e with e words. Track 28

1.

2.

3.

4.

Let's Choose

A. Write a or e.

1.

r__ce

2.

w__ve

3.

c__ke

4.

St__ve

B. Write.

Pete	cave	whale	scene

1.

_____

2.

_____

3.

_____

4.

_____

Let's Read

A. Read, circle, and write the words that rhyme.

1. A <u>grape</u> is on a cape.

cave   these
(grape) wave

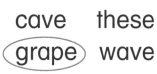

2. A _____ is on the lake.

cake   these
grape   wave

3. The wave is by the _____.

cave   these
grape   cake

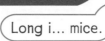
Magic e with i

Magic e makes long i.

Let's Learn

Long i... mice.

A. Listen and speak. Track 29

bike   rice   nine   white   dive

Let's Practice

A. Write.

k__t__   f__v__   r__d__   f__r__

B. Listen and fill the magic e with i words. Track 30

1.
2.
3.
4.
5.

●   ○   ○   ○   ○

C. Listen. Circle or write X. Track 31

1.
2.
3.
4.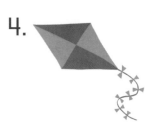

ⓘ   X   i   i

Let's Choose

A. Connect magic e with i words.

Let's Read

A. Read, circle, and write.

kites   five   ride

1. _____ mice dive.

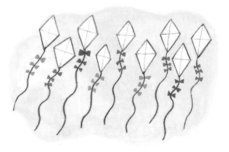

kites   five   ride

2. There are nine white _____.

kites   five   ride

3. I _____ the bike.

Unit 7 Magic e with o

Magic e makes long o.

Long o... hose.

Let's Learn

A. Listen and speak. Track 32

cone

smoke

hole

doze

hose

Let's Practice

A. Write.

p__l__

r__b__

st__n__

b__n__

B. Listen and color. Track 33

 = long o    = not long o

1.

☆

2.

☆

3.

☆

4.

☆

C. Listen for magic e with o. Circle yes or no. Track 34

1.

(yes) no

2.

yes no

3.

yes no

4.

yes no

5.

yes no

Let's Choose

A. Color.

> brown = magic e with o   yellow = magic e with i

1.

2.

3.

4.

5.

6.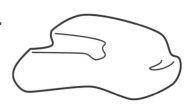

B. Write i or o.

1.

2.

3.

4.

5.

wh__te   f__re   h__le   p__ne   b__ne

Let's Read

A. Read, match, and underline words with long o.

1. The <u>mole</u> is under the cone.   •   •

2. The stove is in a hole.   •   •

3. A stone is next to the pole.   •   •

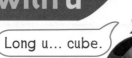

Unit 8 Magic e with u

Magic e makes long u.

Let's Learn

Long u... cube.

A. Listen and speak. Track 35

flute   mule   cube   June

Let's Practice

A. Write.

c__t__   t__n__   pr__n__   J__n__

B. Listen and match. Track 36

1.

2.

3.

6.

→

 u

5.

4.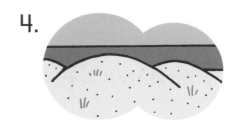

Let's Choose

A. Listen, match, and write. Track 37

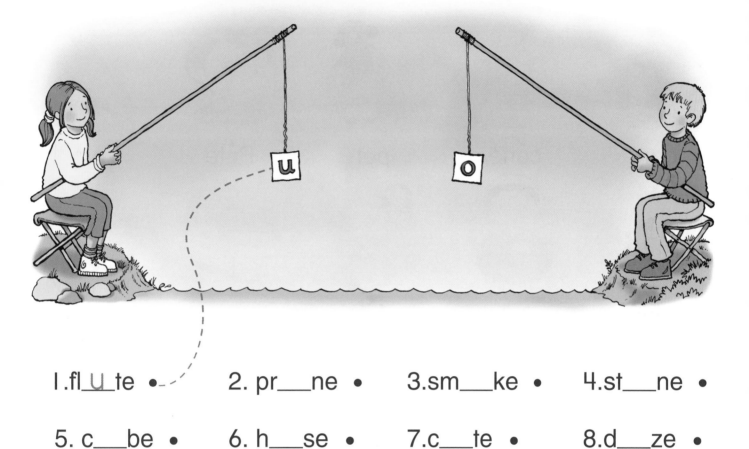

1. fl_u_te •

2. pr___ne •

3. sm___ke •

4. st___ne •

5. c___be •

6. h___se •

7. c___te •

8. d___ze •

Let's Read

A. Read, match, and write.

1. The mule is _____. •

• huge

2. The tube is _____. •

• cube

3. A prune is on the _____. •

• cute

Short u, cub.

Magic e, cube.

Let's Learn

A. Listen and speak. Track 38

can   cane   pet   Pete   pin

pine   Rob   robe   tub   tube

Let's Practice

A. Write and match.

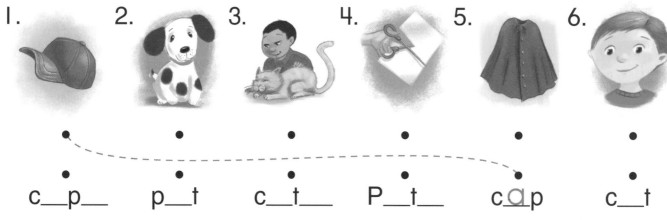

1.   2.   3.   4.   5.   6.

c__p__   p__t   c__t__   P__t__   cap   c__t

B. Listen. Write o, i, or e. Track 39

1.   2.   3.   4.

gl__b   f__n__   gl__b__   f__n

Let's Choose

A. Listen and circle. Track 40

1.

kit kite

2.

hop hope

3.

hug huge

4.

tap tape

B. Listen and circle. Track 41

1.

magic e
not magic e

2.

magic e
not magic e

3.

magic e
not magic e

4.

magic e
not magic e

Let's Read

A. Read and number.

1. Sam is on the tube.
2. The tube is on the can.
3. The can is on the cub.
4. The cub is on the globe.
5. The globe is on the man.

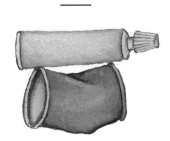

A. Magic e. Write a or e.

1.

2.

3.

4.

5.

_____   _____   _____   _____   _____

B. Magic e. Circle.

1.

2.

3.

4.

5.

e   i   e   i   e   i   e   i   e   i

C. Magic e. Circle words with the same sound.

1. hive

2. cone

D. Magic e. Write o or u and magic e.

1.

2.

3.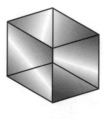

4.

5.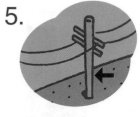

h<u>o</u>s<u>e</u>   sm__k__   c__b__   t__b__   p__l__

E. Magic e. Write a or i.

1.

2.

3.

4.

5.

_____   _____   _____   _____   _____

F. Magic e. Circle.

1.

2.

3.

4.

5.

i   o   i   o   i   o   i   o   i   o

G. Magic e. Write a or u and magic e.

1.

2.

3.

4.

5.

pr__n__   m__l__   l__k__   r__c__   c__k__

H. Magic e. Circle the pairs that rhyme.

1. (wave
   cave)

2. prune
   tune

3. bike
   broke

4. pine
   line

5. cake
   cave

6. hose
   close

7. cute
   flute

8. these
   those

9. stone
   cone

10. fire
    five

1. Find the words. Circle.

```
j  o  c  u  b  e  k  v  w  h  a  l  e  y
b  i  k  e  r  s  u  h  f  i  r  e  t  a
r  o (c  a  k  e) l  k  v  z  m  o  l  e
m  u  l  e  s  t  o  n  e  x  c  d  m  p
x  w  u  l  d  c  d  k  h  n  f  i  v  e
p  r  u  n  e  f  h  t  v  n  i  l  z  u
c  o  n  e  k  m  n  r  x  s  i  d  t  d
p  e  t  e  e  h  e  s  n  a  k  e  o  k
x  d  q  c  u  x  h  q  d  g  r  a  p  e
q  x  e  f  l  u  t  e  h  v  b  y  j  m
```

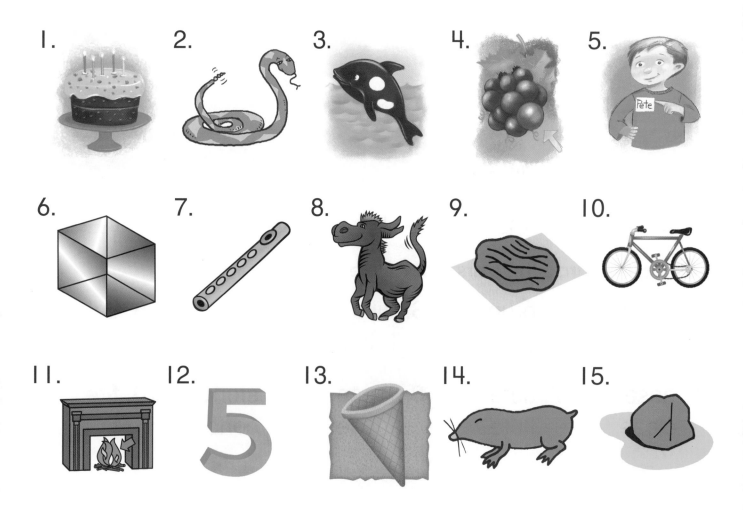

1.   2.   3.   4.   5.

6.   7.   8.   9.   10.

11.   12.   13.   14.   15.

Shark begins with sh.

Fish ends with sh.

Let's Learn

A. Listen and speak. Track 42

shave

shell

ship

wa**sh**

bru**sh**

Let's Practice

A. Write.

____ort

____elf

di____

bu____

B. Begins or ends with sh. Listen and write.  Track 43

1.
sh | ___

2.
___ | sh

3.
___ | ___

4.
___ | ___

5.
___ | ___

6.
___ | ___

7.
___ | ___

8.
___ | ___

Chicken begins with ch.   Sandwich ends with ch.

Let's Learn

A. Listen and speak. Track 44

chin   **ch**eck   bea**ch**   bran**ch**   cou**ch**

Let's Practice

A. Write.

____air   ____ick   pea____   ben____

B. Listen and match. Track 45

2.

3.

1.

| Begins with ch | Ends with ch |

4.

6.

5.

34   Unit 11 / sh and ch

Let's Choose

A. Write ch or sh.

1.
sh

2.
____

3.
____

4.
____

5.
____

6.
____

B. Circle.

1.
ch
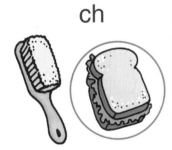

2.
sh

3.
ch

4.
sh

Let's Read

A. Write sh or ch. Read.

1.

A ____eep is on the cou____.

2.

A ____icken is on the ben____.

3.

A ____irt is on the ____ick.

Thin begins with th.

Ruth ends with th.

Let's Learn

A. Listen and speak. Track 46

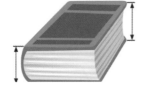

| three | thick | bath | mouth | moth |

Let's Practice

A. Write.

____row   ____irty   too____   boo____

B. Begins or ends with th. Listen and write. Track 47

1.

th|__ __

2.

__ __|th

3.

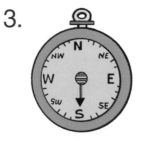

__ __|__ __

4.

__ __|__ __

5.

__ __|__ __

6.

__ __|__ __

7.

__ __|__ __

8.

__ __|__ __

Let's Learn

A. Listen and speak. Track 48

this   **th**at   **th**ese   **th**ose

Let's Practice

A. Write.

____is   ____at   ____ese   ____ose

B. Listen and color. Track 49

> **th = red**   **not th = blue**

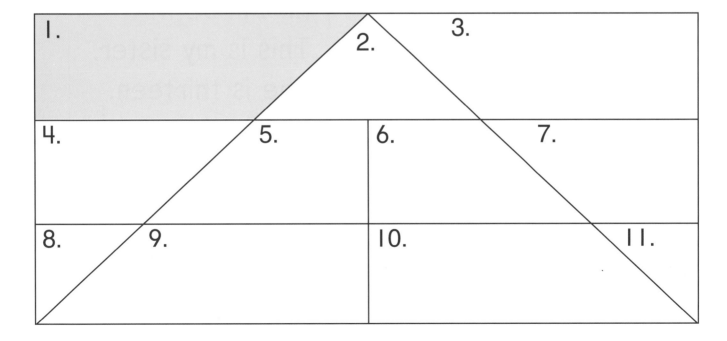

Let's Choose

A. Listen and match. Track 50

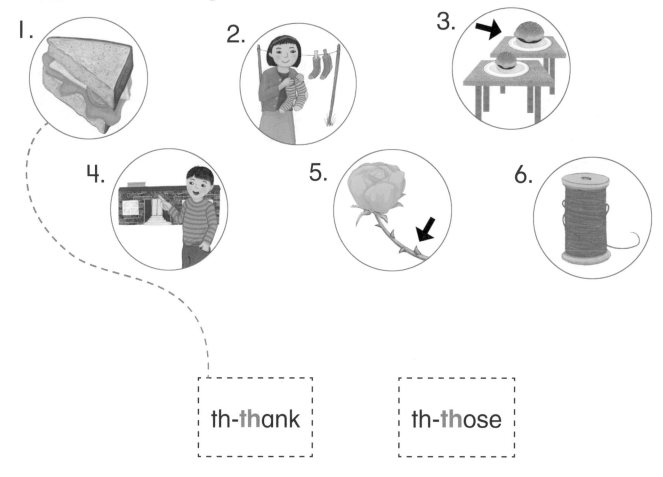

1.

2.

3.

4.

5.

6.

th-**th**ank

th-**th**ose

Let's Read

A. Read and circle th words.

Hi. I'm Beth.
This is my sister.
She is thirteen.
She is thin.

wh and ph

Whale begins with wh.

Let's Learn

A. Listen and speak. Track 51

whisk   white   whale   wheel   whistle

Let's Practice

A. Write.

____eelbarrow   ____isper   ____istle   ____eat

B. Listen and trace. Track 52

 = begins with wh   = doesn't begin with wh

1.
2.
3.
4.

C. Listen. Begins with wh. Circle yes or no. Track 53

1.
2.
3.
4.

yes no   yes no   yes no   yes no

Let's Learn

A. Listen and speak. Track 54

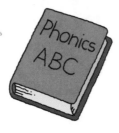

pharmacy   **ph**onics   **ph**one   **ph**oto   **ph**easant

Let's Practice

A. Write.

_____onics   _____easant   _____one   _____armacy

B. Listen and match. Track 55

1.

2.

3.

4.

Let's Choose

A. Circle.

1.
wh ph

2.
wh ph

3.
wh ph

4.
wh ph

B. Circle.

 = ph   = wh

1.
2.
3.
4.
5.

Let's Read

A. Read and circle.

1. Where is the pheasant?
   in the wheelbarrow
   in the wheelchair

2. What is the photo?
   some wheat
   a whale

B. Now count.

How many wh words? _____
How many ph words? _____

A. Begins with sh or ch. Write.

1.

2.

3.

4.

5.

_____   _____   _____   _____   _____

B. Ends with sh or ch. Circle.

1.

2.

3.

4.

5.

sh ch   sh ch   sh ch   sh ch   sh ch

C. th. Circle the words with the same sound.

1. thirty

2. this

3

D. Begins or ends with th. Write.

1.

2.

3.

4.

___ | ___   ___ | ___   ___ | ___   ___ | ___

E. wh or ph. Write.

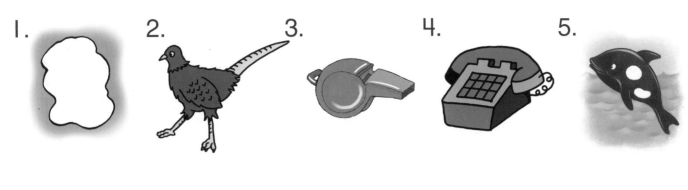

1. _____   2. _____   3. _____   4. _____   5. _____

F. sh or th. Circle.

1. sh th   2. sh th   3. sh th   4. sh th   5. sh th

G. ch or ph. Circle.

1. ch ph   2. ch ph   3. ch ph   4. ch ph   5. ch ph

H. sh, ch, th, wh, or ph. Write.

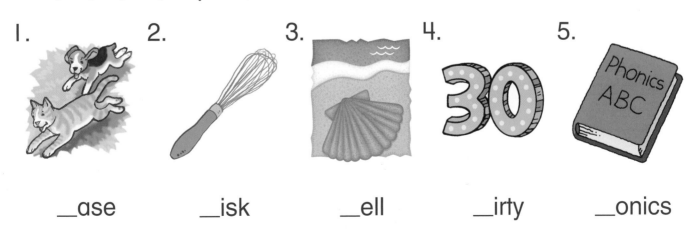

1. __ase   2. __isk   3. __ell   4. __irty   5. __onics

I. Use the code. Write.

1	2	3	4	5	6	7	8	9	10	11	12	13
a	b	c	d	e	f	g	h	i	j	k	l	m
14	15	16	17	18	19	20	21	22	23	24	25	26
n	o	p	q	r	s	t	u	v	w	x	y	z

1.

p	h	o	t	o
16	8	15	20	15

2.

20	8	18	5	5

3.

3	8	1	9	18

4.

20	15	15	20	8

5.

19	8	9	18	20

6.

16	5	1	3	8

7.

20	8	15	18	14

8.

23	8	5	5	12

9.

23	1	19	8

10.

16	8	15	14	5

11.

19	8	5	5	16

12.

13	15	20	8

The Long a Sound

Train is spelled with ai.

Let's Learn

A. Listen and speak. Track 56

rain   paint   snail   train   sail

Let's Practice

A. Write.

br____d   m____l   n____l   ch____n

B. Listen and circle ai words. Track 57

1.    2.   3.   4.    5.

C. Listen and check. Track 58

1.    2.    3.    4.    5.

ai ☐   ai ☐   ai ☐   ai ☐   ai ☐

Hay is spelled with ay.

Let's Learn

A. Listen and speak. Track 59

cl**ay**

tr**ay**

gr**ay**

d**ay**

Let's Practice

A. Write.

p____

h____

pl____

gr____

B. Listen and circle ay words. Track 60

1.
2.
3.
4.
5.
6.

C. Listen and sort. Track 61

ay		not ay		
_ _		_ _ _		

1.
2.
3.
4.
5.

Let's Choose

A. Write.

cake	train	hay	cave

1. _____

2. _____

3. _____

4. _____

B. Circle.

1. ai ay

2. ai ay

3. ai ay

4. ai ay

Let's Read

A. Read and color.

ay = gray	ai = green	magic e = red

1. A | gray | whale | is | in | the | rain.

2. The | nail | is | gray.

3. The | vase | is | on | the | tray.

Queen is spelled with ee.

Jeans is spelled with ea.

Let's Learn

A. Listen and speak. Track 62

b**ea**ch   t**ea**pot   l**ea**f   gr**ee**n   d**ee**r

Let's Practice

A. Write.

ea

s____l   r____d

ee

j____p   sh____p

B. Listen. Circle or write X. Track 63

1.

2.

3.

4.

5.

ea   ea   ea   ea   ea

C. Listen. Circle or write X. Track 64

1.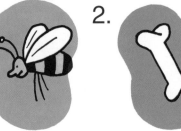

2.

3.

4.

5.

ee   ee   ee   ee   ee

Baby is spelled with y.

He is spelled with e.

Let's Learn

A. Listen and speak. Track 65

| sh**e** | h**e** | cand**y** | sunn**y** | wind**y** |

Let's Practice

A. Write.

m___   w___   cand___   sunn___

B. Underline the words with long e.

1.

2.

3.

C. Listen for words with long e. Fill. Track 66

1.

2.

3.

4.

5.

Let's Choose

A. Match.

1.

2.

3.

4.

5.

- ee
- e
- y
- magic e
- ea

Let's Read

A. Read.

Hi. My name is St**e**ve. Look at m**e**! I am on the b**ea**ch. It's sunn**y**. There is a qu**ee**n. Sh**e** is happ**y**. There is a sh**ee**p, a d**ee**r, and a bunn**y**. I r**ea**d under the tr**ee**.

B. Sort and write.

ea	ee	e	y	magic e
——	——	——	——	——
——	——	——	——	
	——		——	
	——			

Spy is spelled with y.

Let's Learn

A. Listen and speak. Track 67

fry   sky   cry   fly   spy

Let's Practice

A. Write.

fr__   sk__   cr__   fl__   sp__

B. Listen. Write y or X. 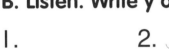 Track 68

1.  2.   3.  4.  5.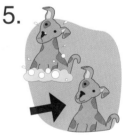

_____   _____   _____   _____   _____

C. Listen and match. Track 69

y

1.  2.  3.  4. 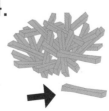 5.

Spies is spelled with ie.

Let's Learn

A. Listen and speak. Track 70

    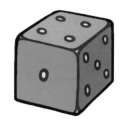

fries   tie   flies   spies   die

Let's Practice

A. Write.

d___   fr___s   sp___s   fl___s   t___

B. Listen. Circle or write X. Track 71

1.

ie

2.

ie

3.

ie

4.

ie

C. Listen and check. Track 72

1.

ie ☐

2.

ie ☐

3.

ie ☐

4.

ie ☐

5.

ie ☐

Let's Choose

A. Write.

pie	kite	fly	tie	fire

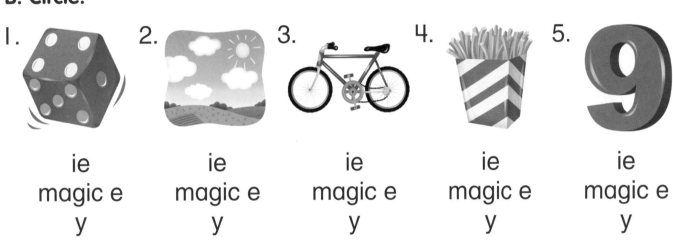

1. _____
2. _____
3. _____
4. _____
5. _____

B. Circle.

1.
   ie
magic e
   y

2.
   ie
magic e
   y

3.
   ie
magic e
   y

4.
   ie
magic e
   y

5.
   ie
magic e
   y

Let's Read

A. Read and circle the long i words.

There are three spies. A spy on a bike eats rice. A spy eats a pie. A spy eats a fry.

Unit 18 The Long o Sound

Doe is spelled with oe.

Coat is spelled with oa.

Let's Learn

A. Listen and speak. Track 73

boat　　　goat　　　hoe　　　Joe　　　doe

Let's Practice

A. Write.

   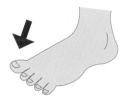

t___d　　　r___d　　　c___t　　　t___

B. Listen and color. Track 74

 oa = long o　　　 = not long o

1.
2.
3.
4.
5.

 oa　　 oa　　 oa　　 oa　　 oa

C. Listen and match. Track 75

oe　　　　　　oe　　　　　　oe

1.
2.
3.

Crow is spelled with ow.

Let's Learn

A. Listen and speak. Track 76

b**ow**l   pill**ow**   sn**ow**   thr**ow**   yell**ow**

Let's Practice

A. Write.

b____   wind____   bl____   cr____

B. Listen for ow. Check or write X. Track 77

1.    2.    3.    4.    5.

[X]   [ ]   [ ]   [ ]   [ ]

C. Listen. Write ow or X. Track 78

1.    2.    3.    4.    5.

_____   _____   _____   _____   _____

Let's Choose

A. Write.

hose	toe	bowl	soap	phone

1. _____

2. _____

3. _____

4. _____

5. _____

B. Color.

1. oa ___ oe

ow magic e

2. oa ___ oe

ow magic e

3. oa ___ oe

ow magic e

4. oa ___ oe

ow magic e

Let's Read

A. Read, number, and circle the words that rhyme.

1.

2.

3.

4.

___ A goat is in a boat.

⊥ A toad is on a road.

___ A mole is next to a pole.

___ A bow is on a crow.

The Long u Sound

Blue is spelled with ue.

Let's Learn

A. Listen and speak. Track 79

clue

blue

glue

fuel

Let's Practice

A. Write.

cl_____

bl_____

gl_____

f_____l

B. Listen and match. Track 80

2.

3.

4.

1.

$\boxed{\text{ue}}$

5.

7.

6.

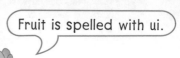

Fruit is spelled with ui.

Let's Learn

A. Listen and speak. Track 81

j**u**ice

cr**ui**se

fr**ui**t

s**ui**t

Let's Practice

A. Write.

j____ce

cr____se

fr____t

s____t

B. Listen. Color or write X. Track 82

1.

2.

3.

4.

5.

6.

Let's Choose

A. Write.

tube	mule	fruit	flute	glue

1. _____

2. _____

3. _____

4. _____

5. _____

B. Color.

★ = ue   ★ = ui   ★ = magic e

1. ☆

2. ☆

3. ☆

4. ☆

Let's Read

A. Read and circle the words that rhyme.

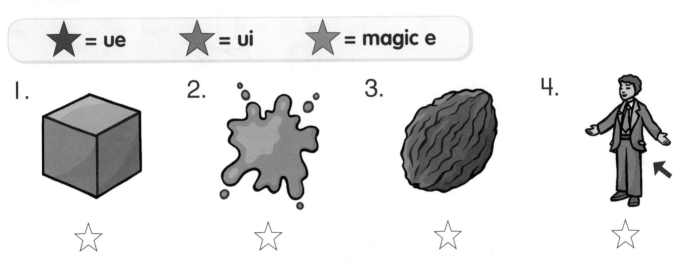

1. A tube is on the cube.

2. The glue is blue.

3. There is fruit on the suit.

A. ai or ay. Write.

1.
_____

2.
_____

3.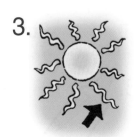
_____

4.
_____

5.
_____

B. ai or ay. Write.

1.
n__l

2.
r__n

3.
h__

4.
p__

5.
tr__n

C. ea or ee. Circle.

1.
ea ee

2.
ea ee

3.
ea ee

4.
ea ee

5.
ea ee

D. e or y. Write.

1.
_____

2.
_____

3.
_____

4.
_____

5.
_____

E. ie or y. Write.

1.  fr___

2.  p___

3.  sk___

4.  fl___

5.  cr___

F. oa, oe, or ow. Write.

1.  _____

2.  _____

3.  _____

4.  _____

5.  _____

G. ue or ui. Circle.

1.  ue ui

2.  ue ui

3.  ue ui

4.  ue ui

5.  ue ui

H. Long vowels. Circle the pairs that rhyme.

1. crow
   bow

2. glue
   blue

3. road
   read

4. green
   queen

5. clay
   spy

6. pay
   hay

7. goat
   boat

8. bunny
   sunny

9. juice
   suit

10. sail
    seal

I. Write.

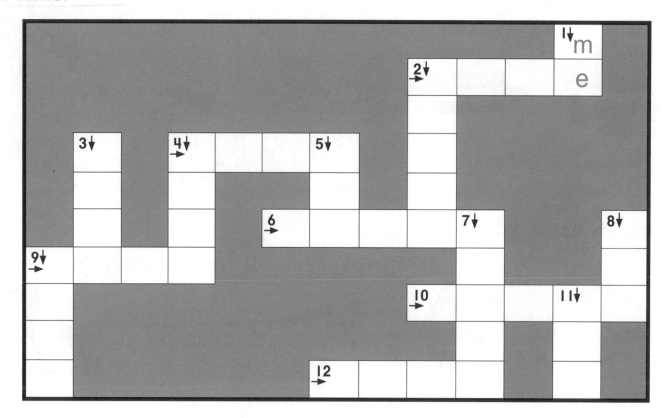

Across

2.
9.
4.
10.
6.
12.

Down

1.
7.
2.
8.
3.
9.
4.
11.
5.